EXTREME JOBS

High-rise Workers

Tony Hyland

MACMILLAN
LIBRARY

First published in 2005 by
MACMILLAN EDUCATION AUSTRALIA PTY LTD
627 Chapel Street, South Yarra 3141

Visit our website at www.macmillan.com.au

Associated companies and representatives throughout the world.

National Library of Australia
Cataloguing-in-Publication data

Hyland, Tony.
High–rise workers.

Includes index.
For middle primary students.
ISBN 0 7329 9811 5.

1. Construction workers – Juvenile literature.
2. Architects and builders – Juvenile literature. I. Title.
(Series: Hyland, Tony. Extreme jobs).

690

Edited by Ruth Jelley
Text and cover design by Peter Shaw
Page layout by SPG
Photo research by Legend Images

Printed in China

Acknowledgements
The author is grateful for the assistance provided by Leighton Construction, Simpson Gumpertz &
Heger Inc., and the Golden Gate Bridge, Highway & Transportation District in arranging interviews
for this book.
The author and the publisher are grateful to the following for permission to reproduce copyright
material:

Cover photograph: At work on high-rise construction site, courtesy of STR/AFP/Getty Images.

Australian Picture Library/Corbis, pp. 13, 16, 18, 22, 23; Coo-ee Picture Library, p. 12; Digital
Vision, p. 26 bottom; Fairfaxphotos/The Age Archives, p. 26 top; Getty Images, pp. 6, 8, 10, 14, 17,
20, 21; Getty Images/Stone, pp. 11, 19, 24; Golden Gate Bridge, p. 29 top; Ged Gross, p. 7; Leighton
Contractors P/L – Spencer Street Station Redevelopment, p. 15 (both); Photodisc, pp. 4, 29 bottom;
Picture Media/Reuters, pp. 5, 28; Picture Media/Reuters/Lyle Stafford, p. 27; Sarah Saunders, p. 30;
STR/AFP/Getty Images, pp. 1, 9; Susan Knack, photo by Brent Gabby, p. 25 bottom; Susan Knack,
photo by William Wayman, p. 25 top.

While every care has been taken to trace and acknowledge copyright, the publisher tenders their
apologies for any accidental infringement where copyright has proved untraceable. Where the
attempt has been unsuccessful, the publisher welcomes information that would redress the situation.

Contents

Glossary words
When a word is printed in **bold**, you can look up its meaning in the Glossary on page 31.

Do you want to be a high-rise worker?

Do you like being up high?

If you enjoy looking down on the world, there might be a job up high for you. Most people like to keep their feet firmly on the ground. For a few others, every day's work starts way above the ground.

Steel workers and crane operators build **skyscrapers**. Architects and engineers work on tall buildings and bridges. Cleaners and painters work hanging from the side of buildings.

Anyone who works up high has an extreme job. The work is often hard. Although the workers take safety precautions, there is a danger of falling. But there is also a thrill in working high above everyone else.

Perhaps you could be a high-rise worker one day.

Construction workers build tall steel buildings.

Working up high

When you work up high, every movement needs extra care. High-rise workers know that any mistake can be deadly.

Workers on modern bridges and building sites take many precautions. In high-rise construction work, cranes erect a large steel 'cage' of protective screens around the top floors. This protects the workers from falls. Workers wear a **safety harness** if they cannot work inside a cage. This is attached to steel cables and hooked on to the steelwork.

Protective barriers and **scaffolding** surround building sites. These stop workers from falling, and also protect people on the ground from falling objects.

Construction workers are kept safe by steel barriers.

5

High-rise work

Most high-rise workers are construction workers. They build tall buildings in cities. As they finish one building, they usually find work on another building.

There are many different workers who work on a construction site. Steel erectors and fixers assemble the steel framework of a building. Crane operators raise and lower the steel beams, and lift other building materials to the building site. Riggers work with the crane operators, making sure that everything is tied securely before it is lifted with the crane.

Building tradespeople, such as bricklayers, carpenters, electricians, plumbers, plasterers and painters also work on the site. Other high-rise workers keep older buildings in good repair. They paint walls, clean windows and repair damaged equipment. They use scaffolds and work platforms to reach the area they are working on.

A rigger indicates to the crane operator where the crane load needs to go.

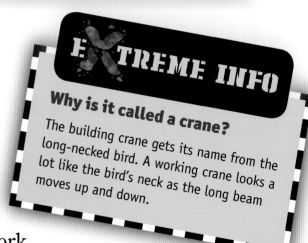

EXTREME INFO

Why is it called a crane?

The building crane gets its name from the long-necked bird. A working crane looks a lot like the bird's neck as the long beam moves up and down.

High-rise safety gear

High-rise construction workers wear practical clothing such as steel-capped work boots and leather gloves. Sometimes they wear overalls to protect their clothes, or padded waterproof jackets to keep warm and dry. They always wear protective gear on building sites, such as:

- a helmet, to protect their heads from falling objects

- warm clothing, to protect against cold weather conditions up high

- a bright yellow or orange reflective vest, to make themselves more visible

- a safety harness, to prevent them from falling.

helmet

reflective vest

warm clothing

safety harness

High-rise workers wear safety gear at all times on construction sites.

Risks and dangers

High-rise workers understand the risks and dangers of their job and take precautions. Some of the risks for high-rise workers are:

Falling   A fall from a great height can be deadly. Workers wear safety equipment such as harnesses and ropes to prevent falls.

Cold   The air is colder up high. It's harder to hold on to tools and equipment with cold, numb fingers.

Wind   Strong winds can blow workers around. **Rope access workers** cannot work in high winds.

Accidents   When accidents happen on a tall building, it is often difficult to get medical help quickly.

Bad weather   Sudden rainstorms can make steel surfaces very slippery. Lightning is also a possible danger.

A high-rise worker wears a safety harness to prevent falls.

A head for heights

People have a natural fear of heights. For some people, this fear is so strong that they become dizzy and lose their sense of balance. This feeling is called vertigo.

People who suffer from vertigo find it impossible to work in high places. High-rise workers know that they could fall and be hurt. But this does not stop them from working. They trust their sense of balance and they have confidence in the safety equipment they use. They understand that they are quite safe, so long as they follow safety procedures. Most high-rise workers enjoy the thrill of being so high above the rest of the world.

High-rise workers are not afraid of being up high.

Training

Workers have to do some training before they can work on a high-rise construction site. They must learn correct safety procedures, such as the use of safety harnesses.

Many high-rise workers are skilled tradespeople. Builders, electricians, painters and many others work as **apprentices** before they become qualified in their trade. Qualified tradespeople need extra training before they can work on high-rise buildings. Most workers learn **first aid**, in case of accidents.

Most other high-rise construction workers learn their skills on the job. Crane operators, steel fixers and riggers do a mix of work and study. They must earn a licence before they are qualified to work.

Apprentices are taught how to do construction work.

EXTREME INFO

Safety matters

Building sites have tough rules. Workers must wear safety gear, such as helmets and reflective vests, at all times. Workers can lose their job for breaking these rules.

Advanced training

Training never really finishes for high-rise workers. As taller and taller buildings are constructed, there are new skills to learn. Engineers design new tools and new ways of fixing steel together.

Crane operators have had to learn new skills because their job has changed so much. Once, a worker called a **dogman** gave directions to crane operators, using whistle blasts. Often, the dogmen rode up and down on the load carried by the crane. This was very dangerous. Today, the job of dogman has changed. Newer and safer work methods have been invented. Crane operators now communicate by radio or even computer.

Experienced workers often go on to study advanced skills. Workers who want to be supervisors learn more about their trade, and also learn how to lead others.

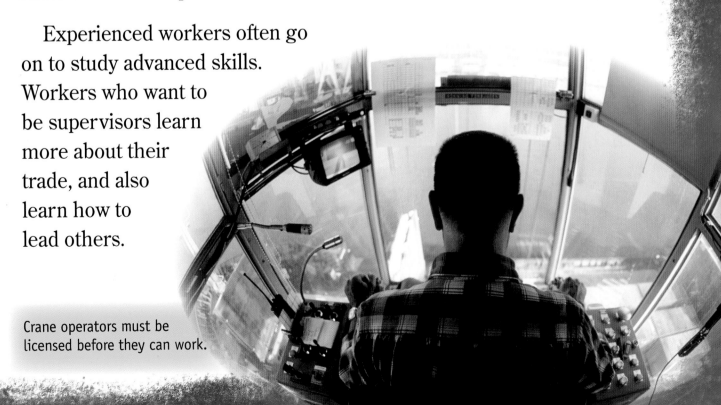

Crane operators must be licensed before they can work.

High-rise history

The first cities developed over 5000 years ago. Workers built tall buildings such as palaces and temples, and high city walls.

Early tall buildings were made of stone or brick. Thousands of years ago, the Egyptians built pyramids with huge blocks of stone. In later times, the Romans built apartment buildings as much as ten storeys high, using brick and timber. Building workers fell and were injured or killed on these jobs. There was no safety equipment, and very little was done to make workers safe. Buildings sometimes fell down because they were poorly made.

Workers built tall cathedrals and palaces 500 to 1000 years ago. They climbed ladders and scaffolds, and even used cranes powered by animals. But there was still very little protection for workers. Building workers simply took care and hoped that they wouldn't fall. They relied on their good balance and good luck.

There was little protection for the builders of this mosque in Iraq.

Skyscrapers

In the 1800s, engineers used steel **girders** to build strong railway bridges. Later, steel girders were used to build the frames for the first true skyscrapers. The first steel-frame skyscraper was built in Chicago in 1884. Many companies continued to build taller and taller skyscrapers. The Empire State Building was built in 1930, in New York City. It was the world's tallest building for many years.

Construction workers had to learn completely new techniques to build these skyscrapers. Huge steel girders were bolted and **riveted** together to form the buildings. Massive cranes were attached to the steel frame to lift girders into place. Worker safety was still a problem. Workers walked around on the bare steel framework. Dogmen rode up and down on crane loads. Deaths and injuries were common.

EXTREME INFO

Taller and taller

The earliest skyscrapers were only about ten storeys high. The Empire State Building was 102 storeys high. It remained the tallest building in the world until 1972.

Workers who built early skyscrapers had little protection and many fell to their deaths.

High-rise jobs

Construction workers

Modern construction workers work in much safer conditions now than in the past. There are still dangers, but workers and building companies have developed safer working methods.

Structural steel erectors are the workers who put together the steel framework. Steel beams and girders are very heavy, so the workers use building cranes, **winches** and **pulleys** to pull each piece into line. Once the pieces are lined up, workers **weld** or rivet them. This joins the pieces permanently. Steel fixers work with the erectors. They cut and shape sections of steel, using bolt cutters and power saws.

The noise of sawing, cutting and hammering on the building site can be deafening. Workers often wear ear protectors to save their hearing.

Steel workers weld the steel framework.

Robert Morabito

Construction worker

Robert Morabito at work on a construction site.

Job

I'm a construction industry **leading hand**.

My work

I make sure things are done safely on the construction site. I fix any safety problems, such as getting machinery moved. If I cannot fix the problem I arrange for somebody who can fix it.

Experience

I've worked on building construction and road-making all of my working life.

Most dangerous work

In my early days, I worked high up on a fully extended ladder, drilling holes in reinforced concrete. It was a dangerous way of doing things. If the drill hit steel, it would stop drilling and twist right around. It could have broken my wrist, or fallen out of my hands. These days we don't work like that, because it's not safe.

Job requirements

Construction workers must have common sense and experience. We need to know how large machinery works, and how to work safely around it.

Robert Morabito works on high-rise buildings.

High-rise jobs

Crane operators

Every tall building site uses tower cranes. Crane operators work slowly and carefully to hoist up the building materials. The cranes hold girders in place while workers rivet them.

Crane operators take special care on windy days, as wind can swing their loads around. Operators must know how much material they can hoist safely. An overloaded crane could topple over, endangering people below. Often, crane operators cannot see the ground or the top floor. Other workers signal by two-way radio that the load is ready to be lifted, or has been unloaded.

Crane operators take care of their own crane. They oil the machinery and check that the **boom** is strong and safe.

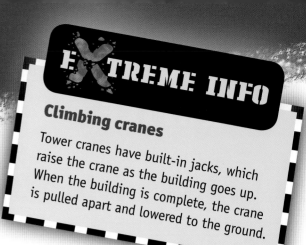

A crane operator works high above a construction site.

Riggers

Riggers work as part of the crane operator's team. They are the workers who assemble loads for the crane to lift. They work with cables, ropes, pulleys and winches. Riggers are experts at tying knots to hold loads together. They learn to **splice** steel cables, joining sections together to make a loading sling. Every crane load can be different. Riggers might have to load some steel girders, followed by a load of concrete panels and then a load of window glass. Each load needs different treatment.

Riggers mainly work on construction sites. But they often find work on ships or in factories, dealing with heavy equipment. Riggers even set up stages and speakers for rock concerts.

RISK FACTOR

Crane operators and riggers learn to deal with risks, such as:

- overloading
- bad weather
- limited visibility.

Riggers guide a steel girder as it is moved with a crane.

High-rise jobs

Building tradespeople

EXTREME INFO

Power supply

Electricians make sure that the workers have a safe power supply for their tools. Construction workers who run long power leads along steel frames could be electrocuted.

Building tradespeople help complete the job once the basic frame of a building is in place. Specialist tradespeople turn the building from a bare frame into a set of comfortable apartments or offices.

There are many different tradespeople who work on high-rise construction sites, including:

- plasterers, who put the internal walls into place

- electricians, who bring electric power into the building. They wire up the main switchboards and then run wires to all of the lights and power points

- glaziers, who install the windows, securing the building against the weather

- plumbers, who lay water and sewerage pipes, and install taps, sinks and toilets

- carpenters, who install wall frames and doors.

A painter applies the finishing touches to a high-rise building by painting the inside walls.

Apprentices

Apprentices work on the job while studying part-time at a technical college. An **apprenticeship** usually takes four years. After that, the apprentice becomes a qualified tradesperson. Apprentices can do further studies in their trade.

Most apprentices are young people, straight out of school. Occasionally an older person will do an apprenticeship, to learn a more interesting or better-paid skill.

Apprentices start with very easy tasks. They learn to keep their working area tidy. Tools and equipment lying on the floor can be dangerous. As the apprentices learn more of their trade, they are allowed to work on more complicated and difficult jobs. Many building trade apprentices work on high-rise buildings.

An apprentice steel worker learning to weld.

RISK FACTOR

Skilled tradespeople and apprentices learn to deal with risks, such as:

- sharp tools
- electric shock
- cluttered workspaces.

High-rise jobs

Architects and engineers

Architects check to see that the building matches their design.

Architects and engineers design buildings. They work in offices, but also spend time on the construction site, making sure the job is done according to their plans.

Architects spend many years at university, learning how to design buildings. Architects must be imaginative and creative, and have a good sense of design. Their buildings must look elegant and attractive.

Architects today design buildings using powerful computer-aided design (CAD) systems. Understanding the small details of how buildings work is a vital part of the architect's job. Airconditioning, water supply and sewerage systems must all work properly. This takes many hours of careful measuring and planning.

EXTREME INFO

Fashion statement

Fashions in architecture change, just as they do with clothes. One hundred years ago, buildings were decorated with elaborate scrolls and carvings. Today, most buildings are very plain and undecorated.

Construction engineers

Construction engineers design the frameworks of buildings, towers and bridges. They make sure that the building is strong enough to support its own huge weight. Engineers take charge of each construction project. They work with architects to make sure that the building matches the design. They also work with the construction supervisors, making sure that the work is done properly.

Construction engineers work with the builders to solve problems.

Engineers spend many years studying at university. They learn about different construction methods, and new building materials. Engineers use computers for some of their work. But they also need to be practical and creative. They work with the construction crew to turn a set of plans into a modern building.

RISK FACTOR

Architects and engineers on construction sites face risks, such as:

- falls
- accidents with machinery
- being hit by falling tools or equipment.

High-rise jobs

Window cleaners

Window cleaners and painters often work from a **swing stage.** This is a strong aluminium platform that is lowered down the side of a building. It is strong enough to support several workers and their equipment.

The swing stage is attached by steel cables to **anchor points** on the roof of the building. It has railings to stop the workers from falling off. Workers control the stage, moving up and down as they finish each section. Swing stages are perfect for jobs that cover large flat areas, such as the face of a skyscraper. They are not so useful for getting into awkward and unusual spots.

Window cleaners wear safety harnesses for extra protection from falls.

EXTREME INFO

Protecting pedestrians

Scaffolding blocks footpaths, causing problems for pedestrians. Scaffolders try to build safe walkways under or around the scaffolding, to protect pedestrians.

Building maintenance methods

Once a building is complete, it needs regular maintenance. Maintenance workers sometimes work on scaffolds. These are sets of pipes and tubes, bolted together on the outside of the building. **Scaffolders** build a strong framework, attaching platforms for workers to stand on. Scaffolds are strong, but they take a long time to erect. For small maintenance jobs, it is easier to send the workers up in a hydraulic lift platform. This looks like a large tub on the end of a crane boom.

Scaffolds and lift platforms rise up from ground level, but they cannot reach to the top of modern skyscrapers. Sometimes it is better to use a swing stage, or rope access methods to work on modern skyscrapers.

RISK FACTOR

Painters and window cleaners depend on their safety equipment. They face risks, such as:

- falls
- overloaded scaffolds or swing stages
- weak anchor points.

These maintenance workers have a strong platform to work on.

High-rise jobs

Rope access workers

Rope access workers use ropes to **rappel** or **abseil** down the sides of buildings. Ropes are attached to strong anchor points and to the worker's harness. Workers can control the speed as they descend the rope.

Rope access workers adapted this system from mountain climbing. They climb to difficult sections of tall buildings, bridges and even oil rigs. Some rope access workers wash windows and brickwork. Others are builders or engineers who check building safety.

Rope access workers are highly trained. They learn many types of knots. Each worker uses two ropes, tied to different anchor points.

Rope access workers can get to places that no other system will reach.

PROFILE

Susan Knack

Structural engineer

Job

I'm a **structural engineer**. I use the rope access method to inspect buildings. I mainly work on walls and roofs – the 'skin' of the building.

Susan Knack prepares to abseil down a building.

Most exciting experience

The most exciting part of my job is solving engineering puzzles. To work out the problems, I need to conduct tests and inspect buildings up close. Rope access is a method I use to inspect buildings.

Favourite thing to do

Once in a while I push off the building, survey the landscape below and enjoy the view. On a sunny day it's great to just hang and take it all in.

Scariest moment

I was rappelling down a tower, 100 metres above the ground, when I slipped. In momentary confusion I squeezed my equipment, which just made me slide down. As soon as I let go, the sliding stopped. Nothing was hurt but my pride.

Susan Knack uses rope access equipment in her job as a structural engineer.

Bridge disaster

In 1970, a section of a bridge in Melbourne collapsed during construction. It crashed to the ground, killing 35 workers. The section was badly designed, and could not hold its own weight.

Bridge builders and ironworkers

No two bridges are ever exactly the same. Bridges can cross harbours, swampy rivers, or narrow rocky canyons. Building a bridge needs the skills of many different workers.

Construction engineers design each bridge differently. They call on engineers from around the world for advice. Experts examine the rock and soil where the bridge will stand. The ground must be strong enough to support the bridge.

Steel workers, **ironworkers**, crane operators and concreters all come to work on the bridge. Their work is similar to ordinary construction jobs, but they have to learn some new methods as well.

It will take a long time to finish constructing these bridges.

Bridge maintenance

Steel bridges are strong, but they can rust and corrode. Bridge ironworkers keep the steel sections of a bridge in good working order. They check every steel plate and rivet, replacing any that have **corroded**. They use cutting and welding tools to replace steel sections.

Ironworkers work with bridge painters. They use a swing stage or scaffold, but occasionally they need to climb around on the steel structure of the bridge. They wear two safety cables, attached to different sections of steelwork.

Ironworkers rig the swing stage for the painters, and then move the stage to a new area when it is needed. They remove steel plates to let the painters work inside the hollow sections of the bridge. The two groups work together as a team.

RISK FACTOR

Bridge workers often work in difficult and dangerous conditions. They must deal with:

- falls
- wet and windy weather
- burns and cuts caused by steel-cutting equipment.

Bridge maintenance workers use scaffolding when working on the bridge.

High-rise jobs

Bridge painters

Bridge painters help to maintain the steel structures of bridges. Bridges such as San Francisco's Golden Gate Bridge and the Sydney Harbour Bridge are famous landmarks throughout the world, and must be maintained regularly.

Bridge painters crawl around the huge structures of steel bridges, cleaning and painting. On large bridges, this work never finishes.
Paint teams inspect the bridge and work out a plan to paint the whole bridge over several years.

Bridge painters work from a swing stage on the Sydney Harbour Bridge.

Bridge painters work from a swing stage. This holds all of their gear. Their safety lines are firmly attached to the bridge steel. They sometimes climb around on the bridge itself to reach tricky spots.

EXTREME INFO

Mini-climates

The Golden Gate Bridge is so long that different parts of it have different weather. The north end is sheltered by hills, but the south end is exposed to salty sea air, and corrosion is more severe.

PROFILE

Dennis 'Rocky' Dellarocca

Bridge painter

Rocky Dellarocca, at work on the Golden Gate Bridge.

Job

I'm the Bridge Paint Superintendent of the Golden Gate Bridge, USA.

Experience

I've worked on bridges since I was 20 years old. I did a bridge painting apprenticeship. Now I'm in charge of about 30 bridge painters. I still go out 'on the steel' nearly every day. 'On the steel' is our term for working on the bridge.

My work

We work in teams of six. We wear a full body harness, like a parachute harness. Each person has their own steel safety line, hooked to the full body harness.

Bad weather

We can't work on the steel if it is wet and slippery, or if the wind is really strong. At those times we stay inside, maintaining our spray-guns and spray-pots. As soon as the weather clears up, we're ready to get out and start work.

Why I work on the bridge

I love this job. The Golden Gate Bridge is a world icon. We're taking care of something very special here.

Teams of painters work to keep the Golden Gate Bridge in top condition.

Could you be a high-rise worker?

You could be a high-rise worker if you:

- have normal health

- are physically fit

- have a good head for heights

- enjoy being active outdoors

- are adventurous

- can be responsible and work as part of a team.

If you learn a trade, such as welding or painting, construction companies will want to employ you.

If you prefer, you could study engineering or architecture. You could spend a lot of time climbing around tall buildings.

Try indoor climbing, or abseiling classes. If you like that, you might have an exciting job in the future.

Rock climbing is a good way to practise your climbing and abseiling skills.

Glossary

abseil	to climb using safety ropes
anchor points	safe points to attach ropes
apprentices	people who learn a trade while working at it
apprenticeship	period of being an apprentice
boom	long beam section of a crane
corroded	rusted or decayed away
dogman	a construction worker who signals to the crane operator
first aid	the first help given to an injured person
girders	large supporting beams
ironworkers	workers trained in cutting and welding steel
leading hand	leader of a small team of workers
pulleys	grooved wheels used with a rope or cable to lift heavy objects
rappel	to climb using safety ropes
riveted	held together by strong steel pins
rope access workers	workers who use climbing ropes
safety harness	set of strong straps, to attach to safety cables
scaffolders	workers who build scaffolding
scaffolding	temporary structure often built using pipes and planks
skyscrapers	very tall buildings made with a steel frame
splice	to join two sections of rope or steel cable
structural engineer	engineer trained in constructing steel frame buildings
swing stage	strong work platform hung from side of building or bridge
weld	to join two pieces of metal with intense heat
winches	machines that hoist heavy objects by winding a cable around a drum

Index